FLAVORS OF THE WORLD

THE FOOD OF
GREECE

Tamra B. Orr

mc **Marshall Cavendish**
Benchmark
New York

Other Marshall Cavendish Offices:
Marshall Cavendish International (Asia) Private Limited, 1 New Industrial Road, Singapore 536196 • Marshall Cavendish International (Thailand) Co Ltd. 253 Asoke, 12th Flr, Sukhumvit 21 Road, Klongtoey Nua, Wattana, Bangkok 10110, Thailand • Marshall Cavendish (Malaysia) Sdn Bhd, Times Subang, Lot 46, Subang Hi-Tech Industrial Park, Batu Tiga, 40000 Shah Alam, Selangor Darul Ehsan, Malaysia

Marshall Cavendish is a trademark of Times Publishing Limited
All websites were available and accurate when this book was sent to press.

Library of Congress Cataloging-in-Publication Data
The food of Greece / Tamra B. Orr.
  p. cm. — (Flavors of the world)
Includes bibliographical references and index.
Summary: "Explore the culture, traditions, and festivals of Greece through its food"—Provided by publisher.
ISBN 978-1-60870-235-0 (print)   ISBN 978-1-60870-688-4 (ebook)
  1. Food habits—Greece—Juvenile literature. 2. Festivals—Greece—Juvenile literature. 3. Greece—
    Social life and customs—Juvenile literature. I. Title.
GT2853.G8077 2012
394.1'209495—dc22
2010035820

Editor: Christine Florie
Publisher: Michelle Bisson
Art Director: Anahid Hamparian
Series Designer: Kay Petronio

Expert Reader: Carol Helstosky, Associate Professor, European Cultural History, University of Denver, Denver, Colorado

Photo research by Marybeth Kavanagh
Cover photo by Hemis/Alamy
The photographs in this book are used by permission and through the courtesy of: *Alamy*: Terry Harris/ just greece photo library, 4, 42; LOOK Die Bildagentur der Fotografen GmbH, 9; Nicholas Pitt, 11; National Geographic Image Collection, 14; IML Image Group Ltd, 23, 53; Simon Reddy, 30; Mikko Mattila-Commercial Collection, 31; Samuel Lord, 33; Elaine Rhodes, 34; Bon Appetit, 40; Eye Ubiquitous, 46; MARKA, 49; Aurora Photos, 51; Images Etc Ltd., 54; *The Image Works*: Hervé Champollion/akg-images, 8; Mary Evans Picture Library, 16; Werner Stuhler/Sueddeutsche Zeitung Photo, 58; *Landov*: Roland Holschneider/dpa, 18; Amy Becker/MCT, 19; *SuperStock*: Stock Connection, 20; IML, 25; Lonely Planet, 26; Food and Drink, 27, 35; Imagebroker.net, 36; Photocuisine, 38; age fotostock, 39; *Fotolia*: Akhilesh Sharma (banner), cover, 1, 3, 4, 17, 32, 44, 54; Sandra Cunningham (spices), 12, 24, 41, 47, 56; Chiyacat (eggplant), front & back covers, 1, 64; Andrey Kiseley (kabob), 3; *Shutterstock*: Suto Norbert Zsolt (map), cover, 1, 2, 28, 36, 45, 52, 55, 57; *VectorStock*: nice monkey (plate), back cover, 3

Maps (pp. 6 and 22) by Mapping Specialists Limited

Printed in Malaysia (T)

135642

CONTENTS

ONE

Welcome to Greece!

||||||||||||||||||||||||||||||||||||||||||||||||||||||||||||||||||||||||||||||||||||||||||

Tucked onto the bottom of southern Europe is the country of Greece and its thousands of islands. At just under 51,000 square miles (132,089 square kilometers), it is about the size of Alabama. Home to over 11 million people, this unique land manages to share borders with four countries and touch on three different seas. The neighbors of Greece on its northern border are Albania, Macedonia, and Bulgaria. Trailing along its western side is the Ionian Sea, while the Mediterranean Sea curves around the southern border, and the Aegean Sea and Turkey lie to the east.

Over the centuries, Greece has been a popular stop on seagoing journeys. As a result, many new foods and spices from other lands have become a part of the national cuisine. As long ago as

A bounty of drink and freshly prepared food is enjoyed at this Greek table.

TOPOGRAPHICAL MAP OF GREECE

BULGARIA

MACEDONIA

TURKEY

ALBANIA

Mt. Olympus

Corfu

IONIAN ISLANDS

GREECE

PINDUS MTS.

SPORADES ISLANDS

Lesbos

Aegean Sea

NORTH EAST AEGEAN ISLANDS

TURKEY

Evia

Hios

Kefalonia

Athens

Samos

Zakynthos

Corinth Canal

PELOPONNESE

Aegina

Ionian Sea

Poros

Spetses   Hydra

CYCLADES ISLANDS

SARCONIC GULF ISLANDS

DODECANESE ISLANDS

Crete

Mediterranean Sea

the sixth century, ships full of people from India and Asia Minor used the trade routes that entered the seas surrounding Greece. The foods the traders brought with them—new spices and exotic vegetables and meats—soon became part of the Greek diet.

Over the centuries, Greeks have used some of the recipes of visitors from other lands, often incorporating the seafood so plentiful in its coastal waters, to create foods that are simple yet reflective of the nation's history.

The Art of Eating

The word *gastronomy* means the art of selecting, preparing, serving, and eating food. Where did the word come from? Ancient Greece! One of the first known cookbooks was written in the fifth century BCE by a Greek poet named Archestratus. Its title, *Gastronomia*, means "rules for the stomach." The cookbook was written like a poem. In more than three hundred verses, it described the best food and drink of the time and gave directions for preparing it. Very little of this cookbook survives today, but the word Archestratus chose for his book is still used in cooking and for many articles and blogs about food.

Landforms

Greece is usually thought of in three parts: the mainland in the north, a **peninsula** called the Peloponnese, and about two thousand islands, of which only a small percentage have people living on them. With almost two-thirds of Greece covered in mountains and rocks, finding fertile soil for planting crops has never been easy. The country's landscape itself limits what can be grown there. Many Greek recipes focus on using few ingredients, such as olives, grapes, and wheat, combined in

Farms are found in the fertile valleys of Macedonia, a region in northern Greece.

as many different ways as possible. Historically, most farmers chose to live in coastal areas, where the soil was better. Others sought the more fertile valleys and plains of Thessaly, the northern Greek province of Macedonia (not to be confused with today's Republic of Macedonia), and the Thrace region because there the rain would pool, making it

Goats are well suited for the rocky slopes of Greece.

easier to grow crops like figs, grain, and grapes.

The rocky terrain of Greece also explains why the dairy products found in the Greek diet do not come from cows, but from goats. Goats are far better able to handle living in the mountains than cattle. For the same reason, beef is rarely used in recipes, but sheep, which are accustomed to living in hilly areas, are much more commonly raised for meat as well as for wool.

The tallest mountain in all of Greece, with a height of 9,570 feet (2,916 meters), is Mount Olympus—famed from countless ancient stories, or myths, for which the country is known. Many tales say Mount Olympus was the home of the gods, including the all-powerful Zeus and his wife, Hera. A chain of mountains called the Pindus Mountains reaches from the northwest part of the mainland all the way to the Peloponnese, the peninsular region.

The Peloponnese looks a little like a four-fingered hand pointing out to the sea. It is separated from the mainland by the Corinth Canal. This man-made waterway was completed in the summer of 1893 by a crew of French, Greek, and Hungarian workers. The idea for a canal across the Peloponnese was thousands of years old, but the ancient Greeks and Romans had not succeeded in bringing their plans to completion. The Corinth Canal is just under 4 miles (6.4 km) long and a little over 80 feet (24.38 m) wide. This relatively small waterway did a great deal to cut down the time ships needed to traverse the region. By being able to sail through the canal instead of having to go around the peninsula, ships shortened their journeys by 200 miles (321 km)—or several days of sailing. The time the sailors gained encouraged them to stop and rest—and share their food and drink with the Greeks. Today's huge cargo ships cannot fit through the Corinth Canal, but it is still used by smaller vessels.

Although Greece has thousands of islands scattered across the surrounding seas, only about 170 of them have people living on them. The Ionian Islands in the west are green and the soil is rich. Since Kefalonia, Corfu, and Zakynthos were under Italian control for hundreds of years, their cuisine includes pasta, peppers, and tomatoes.

Other groups of islands include the Sarconic Islands, where you will find Aegina, one of the largest of the group, as well as Poros, Hydra, and Spetsai. The Sporades Islands are a numerous group, but only the three largest islands are inhabited. The Cyclades are more heavily populated: out of a total of thirty-nine islands, twenty-four have people living on them. Many of the Cyclades Islands are dry and rocky. The Dodecanese Islands are in the southeast part of the Aegean Sea, only a ferry ride away from Turkey. The North East Aegean Islands include Samos, Hios, and Lesbos.

A salad of tomatoes and peppers is prepared for a beach lunch on the Ionian Islands.

Ladolemono
(Lemon and Olive Oil Sauce)

It is almost impossible to eat anything in Greece without tasting this sauce. It is made from the country's two favorite ingredients: olive oil and lemon juice. It goes over hot and cold food and vegetables or meat. It is a sauce, a marinade, and a salad dressing. Because ladolemono tastes best when it has just been prepared and loses a great deal of freshness when left in the refrigerator, you should make only enough for the current meal. With a little help from an adult, you can put the sauce together at the very last minute.

Ingredients

4 tablespoons extra-virgin olive oil

2 tablespoons freshly squeezed lemon juice

Salt to taste

Dash of pepper

Dash of oregano (optional)

Directions

Pour the olive oil into a bowl. Add the lemon juice. Whisk the two together. Add salt and pepper. Add the optional oregano if you like.

Pour it all into a jar and shake well. Serve!

Climate

Although in many parts of the world there are huge changes in temperature and in rainfall or snowfall from one season to the next, all of Greece tends to share the same climate. Being so close to the Mediterranean Sea, it is subtropical, meaning that the summers are long, hot, and dry, and the winters short and mild. The only snow tends to be in the highest mountains, and rain is limited year round. Weather like this is perfect for tourists hoping to swim in the ocean and get a tan—but terrible for the farmers trying to grow many of the crops that thrive elsewhere in Europe. When early settlers in the area now called Greece realized that olive trees could grow well in the climate they found, they were one large step closer to creating the food that the entire country would one day be known for—olives.

History

Greece has one of the oldest cultures in the world. In fact, some people refer to the country as the birthplace of European civilization. Many visitors to Greece enjoy the food—but their main reason for coming is to see the famous ancient ruins. Athens, the capital of Greece, has the rock of Acropolis, which dates all the way back to the fifth century, the time of the fall of the Roman Empire. It is on the Acropolis that the Parthenon, a temple that was once dedicated to the goddess Athena, is located. Considered one

Early Greeks harvest olives and press them for oil.

of the most important pieces of architecture in the world, the temple inspired countless other religious, government, and privately owned buildings with its columns and pillars. Other buildings throughout parts of Greece are even more ancient—as old as four thousand years. Standing inside these ruins is like stepping back in time.

An Unusual Crime

In ancient Greece, it was a crime—punishable by death—to cut down an olive tree. Even today, the government gives workers paid leave when they have to miss work in November to harvest their olive crops.

Greece is also the birthplace of some of the most important developments in the world. The philosophers Plato and Socrates came from there. The Greek myths that recount tales of great adventure and bravery involving gods, goddesses, and heroes started there. Homer, among other authors, told these stories in works such as *The Iliad* and *The Odyssey*. In addition, ancient Greeks made many important contributions to everything from mathematics to competitive sports.

One thing the ancient Greeks did not have was a strong military force, and because of that, over the years, they were invaded repeatedly. First it was Philip II of Macedon, then the Romans. Each time the land was invaded, the new culture brought spices that remain part of Greek cooking today. When the armies of Alexander the Great came through, they brought nutmeg and cinnamon. During the four hundred years the Ottoman Turks ruled the area, they introduced beans, spinach,

The ancient Greeks are known for their many contributions. This illustration depicts an ancient Greek banquet.

coffee, and rice. Other visitors—or invading armies—brought barley and wheat and others meat such as lamb, pork, and goat. Even as the land changed hands from one leader to the next, one group to another, the flavors that would come to represent the Greece of today were growing in number.

TWO

In the Land of Liquid Gold

Throughout Greece, one can find ingredients that are a part of almost every dish that is prepared. From many types of olives, as well as olive oil, ripe tomatoes, lemon juice, and feta cheese, the people make everything from snacks to main dishes to salads to desserts, and even holiday treats.

Liquid Gold

When Greece is referred to as the land of "liquid gold," you may think it sounds like a place people would go in search of a fortune. In this country, however, the term means something entirely different. In Greece, liquid gold is olive oil. It is no wonder the Greeks think this oil is so valuable. It is added to virtually everything they cook or eat.

Olives are the supreme food in Greece. All in all, more than 100 million olive trees grow throughout the country. Olive trees are hardy—they can live as long as six hundred years. The olive

An olive grove thrives on the Greek island of Zakynthos, the third largest of the Ionian Islands.

is the national symbol. It has been part of the people's daily recipes for thousands of years. Each year, millions of groves produce more than 120,000 tons of olives, in more than a hundred varieties. One-third of the crop stays in Greece, while the rest is exported to many other countries.

Olives come in all shapes, colors, textures, and sizes. The Greek greens, for example, are firm and crunchy. The amphissas are brown and soft, with a mild flavor. The kalamata is dark, large, and bitter. The Nafplion, or cracked olive, is green and slightly bitter and is often flavored with garlic and lemon. Olives from the island of Chios are flavored with lemon, orange juice, and the licorice-flavored leaves of the mastic tree. Olives of all types, however, must be **cured**, or soaked in brine before they are eaten.

A vendor offers dozens of varieties of olives at a street stand in Athens.

How are olives used? It might be easier to say how they are not! The most important use is in making olive oil. In addition, olives are put in pies, bread, pastes, sauces, salads, and snacks. Once picked, the olives from which oil will be extracted are ground into a paste. The paste is then pressed between large millstones or steel drums, to extract, or press out, the oil. The first oil to be extracted from the harvested olives is "extra-virgin olive oil." It is considered the best of all. This liquid gold is used in frying,

A shop on the island of Corfu sells several Greek olive oils.

marinating, rubbing, and flavoring food. Every single Greek on average consumes 7 gallons of it every year—more than any other group in the world. Chances are that almost every Greek recipe will call for olive oil in one way or another—butter is almost never used, or any other kind of **shortening** or oil.

The perfect partner for olive oil, most Greeks would say, is lemon juice, a close second to olives in the national cuisine. Lemons were not native to the area but have been grown there since 1000–1200 CE when Middle Eastern traders brought them from Turkey. The Greeks strongly believe in the idea of balance in their food, and the combination of olive oil and lemon juice is a great example. The two flavors—and their textures—go very well together, and a mixture of olive oil and lemon juice is used for everything from salad dressings to toppings for vegetables to sauces for meat. Lemon juice is also sometimes used as medicine to help people feel better. Since lemons have high levels of vitamin C, there may be a good reason for the practice.

Mainland Greece

The mainland of Greece is the largest part of the country. It has the greatest diversity in topography and food. Since this region has green pastures, sheep and goats are able to graze. Both are eaten as meat, and their milk is used for making feta cheese and yogurt. The rich soil lends itself to crops such as potatoes, eggplant, onions, spinach, corn, and beans. The hillsides support the endless groves of olive trees.

THE FOOD REGIONS of GREECE

GREECE

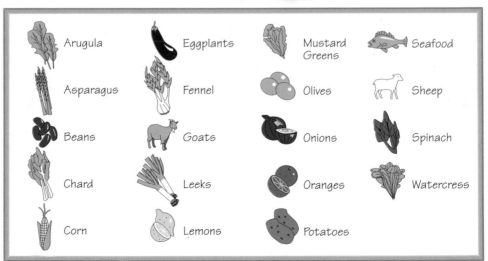

Arugula		Eggplants		Mustard Greens		Seafood
Asparagus		Fennel		Olives		Sheep
Beans		Goats		Onions		Spinach
Chard		Leeks		Oranges		Watercress
Corn		Lemons		Potatoes		

In addition, thanks to extra spring rains on the mainland, many hillsides are covered with what the Greeks call *horta*, or wild greens. Among more than three hundred different kinds of greens that grow throughout the countryside are leeks, asparagus, fennel, arugula, chard, mustard greens, and watercress. Farmers who specialize in growing these greens sell them to small markets and large grocery stores. Some families, however, prefer to spend an afternoon or two every week picking wild greens directly from the fields.

Hundreds of varieties of greens grow throughout Greece.

Horiatiki
(Greek Village Salad)

This salad is a wonderful example of what makes Greek dishes fresh and unique. It is easy to prepare for a few people—or to double or triple for company. The fresher and riper the tomatoes, the better the salad will taste. Make sure an adult helps you with the slicing and dicing.

Ingredients

4 tomatoes

1 small, sweet onion

1 green bell pepper

1 cucumber

1 cup black olives

⅓ pound feta cheese (crumble it into small pieces)

¼ cup olive oil

1 teaspoon oregano

½ teaspoon garlic powder (optional)

Directions

Cut each tomato into five or six slices. Slice the onion into thin rounds. Remove the seeds from the green pepper and cut it into thin rings. Peel the cucumber and cut it into thin slices.

Combine the tomatoes, onion, pepper, and cucumber in a large salad bowl. Add the black olives and feta cheese. Add the olive oil, oregano, and the optional garlic powder if you like.

Toss the salad. Serve right away!

In Greece, greens are used in an amazing number of ways, not just in salads. They are ingredients in stews and soups and even porridges. Some are mixed with flour and then fried in hot oil as patties. Others are lightly steamed and topped with the Greeks' favorite sauce of olive oil and lemon juice.

Mainland Greece includes the northern province of Macedonia. Because of the extensive seacoast, one of the region's favorite dishes features shrimp baked in a tomato and feta cheese sauce. The area is also known for its delicate pastries and syrup-soaked cakes, both of which are often prepared in wood-burning ovens.

The mainland is famous for the city of Athens, the Greek capital, home to 750,000 people. The city's outdoor Central Market, over a hundred years old, is one of the largest markets in all of Europe. Row after row of vendors sell their specialties in their stalls, calling out to advertise the freshness of

A sweet shop worker in Macedonia prepares local favorite pastries.

A vendor sells meat at the Athens Central Market.

their fruits and vegetables. Poultry, seafood, and beef are also displayed in stalls. Some vendors sell dried herbs, nuts, and sweets, and still others offer prepared food for those who want to eat while they shop.

On the Peninsula

More kalamata olives are grown on the Peloponnese than anywhere else in the world. There the kalamata olive tree is king.

These olives are mahogany brown, almost black. They are shaped like almonds and have a strong, bitter flavor. In this region, orange and lemon groves, as well as crops of eggplant, artichokes, and figs thrive.

The Peloponnese is known for its salted pork, as well. How it is prepared depends on the part of the peninsula it comes from. In the mountainous area, meat from the thighs of pigs is salted,

Kalamata olives are grown on the Peloponnese.

Rodhozahari (Rose Petal Jam)

One of Greece's best kept secrets is the rose petal jam made at the Taxiarhon Monastery in the northeastern part of the Peloponnese. For centuries, monks have lived in this walled complex, making a special treat from the petals of beautiful flowers. They have to work hard because they only have about three weeks—from the end of May to the middle of June—to pick their roses.

The rose gardens themselves are hidden from view, and only the monks are allowed to go into them. The brothers spend hours collecting and cleaning 200 pounds of rose petals each day of the season. They are often out at sunrise to avoid the heat of the afternoon. The petals are pulled off and collected in barrels. Then, in batches of just over 20 pounds, the petals are mixed with sugar, citric acid, and water. The monks mash everything all together for about 20 minutes until it turns into a dark purple pulp. Then the mash is placed in barrels and refrigerated. When the monks get an order for jam, they heat a quantity of the pulp until it becomes a thick syrup and add some lemon juice. They allow the mixture to simmer and finally put it into jars to be shipped out. The jam has a light, sweet flavor that is loved throughout the country. It is eaten with a spoon as a special treat.

boiled in wine, browned in olive oil, and then spiced with cinnamon and pepper. Finally, it is stored in olive oil until it is time to use it in a recipe. In another region, pork is smoked over sage or cypress wood and then boiled with oregano and orange peel. Pork sausages are made with many spices such as garlic, nutmeg, and allspice.

Throughout the Islands

With some 170 inhabited islands spread out across the trio of seas around Greece, the traveler can find all kinds of food and cooking styles. Some of the islands are extremely popular tourist stops. They tend to cater to international visitors rather than offering genuine but simple Greek recipes. Some islands feature dishes their own people love—but residents of the next island over may never have heard of them. Some dishes are based on Italy's cooking styles—using a lot of tomatoes and pasta, while others still show signs—such as spicy peppers—of the years during which the Greek isles were ruled by the Turks.

On the island of Corfu, in the Ionian Sea, a stew of meat and vegetables called *stuffato* is popular, as is *tsigarelli*, a mix of sautéed greens with lots of garlic and hot red peppers. Evia, in the Aegean Islands, offers fried cheese bread, and the Albanians who have moved to the area brought along their recipe for spicy meatballs. In the North East Aegean Islands, just off the coast of Turkey, seafood is always offered, including exotic dishes like boiled skate's fin and rolled monkfish fillet. The islands of the Cyclades are generally dry and rocky, so cooks have to be unusually creative. Favorite ingredients here include barley, chickpeas, and fava beans; wheat biscuits are popular, as well.

The cuisine of Greece changes from one location to another, depending on how easy it is to grow crops, how many

Stuffato is a popular Greek stew of meat and vegetables.

Fresh octopus, a favorite meal in Greece, dries in the sun.

animals can graze comfortably on the land available, and what seafood can be caught nearby. However, the attitude toward food—and the entire country's devotion to the olive—stays the same from one end of the country to the other.

THREE

A Day in Greece

In Greece, some believe a guest who stops by might actually be a god in disguise, so it's a good idea to treat him or her well. Because of this old superstition, or because the people are naturally hospitable, guests are always welcomed at the Greek family table, and an extra plate is eagerly filled and shared. Having someone stop by to eat is considered an honor, and family members will happily make do with small servings to be sure that the guest has enough. Anyone who might refuse to accept an invitation to a meal would only succeed in hurting the feelings of the would-be hosts. Such an insult would not be easily forgiven or forgotten. In Greece, how food is eaten and who one shares it with is as important as the food itself.

Breakfast in Greece is often eaten early, especially by farmers. Their first meal of the day is almost always light, perhaps nothing more than a strong cup of Turkish coffee or a cup of hot tea. The farmer will eat his lunch out in the field. His basket of food might include hot soup, bread and cheese, slices of tomatoes and cucumbers—and of course some olives. Dessert is rare, although it might be a piece of fresh fruit. For the city dweller, lunch is more often eaten late and blends right into a **siesta**, or rest period. Dinner for the farmer comes after sundown and usually centers on some type of meat, while city dwellers often don't sit down to dine until 10 p.m. It is not unusual for families to eat at long, wooden tables.

In Greece, breakfast is a light meal of coffee and sometimes a pastry.

Traditional bread making takes place in a communal oven.

Meals are prepared at outdoor ovens. In some small villages, women who don't have their own ovens will walk their pots down to the local baker and use his ovens once his loaves are finished.

In between meals, many Greeks eat snacks, or *mezedes*, prepared by their families or bought from street vendors. In addition, many men end their day at a coffeehouse. There they drink strong coffee, eat sweet snacks, and discuss politics and other issues. Some will even lean back in the chair and take a nap or listen to music.

Layer after Layer

In Greece, recipes are often passed down from generation to generation. One of the most popular recipes for a mother to teach her daughter is how to make *phyllo*, a paper-thin pastry dough used throughout the country in many desserts, as well as in appetizers and main dishes.

Baklava is a Greek dessert made with layers of phyllo.

The Evil Eye

Look around some traditional Greek homes and you might spy garlic and onions hanging in the corners. They are not there for cooking but to help ward off the evil eye or *matiasma*, a look from another person that can make the one who was targeted feel sick or depressed. To protect themselves from the evil eye, some Greeks rely on displays of garlic and onions. Others wear a little blue marble glass with an eye painted on it or a special blue bracelet.

Making phyllo is challenging. The dough itself contains flour, water, salt, lemon juice, and—naturally—olive oil. It has to be mixed properly and then rolled out again and again with a rolling pin until it is as thin as a piece of paper. In dishes like *baklava*, professional bakers may use as many as forty or fifty layers of this dough. Baklava is a dessert consisting of layers of phyllo, between which are spread such ingredients as chopped walnuts, pistachios, almonds, and pine nuts, plus cloves, sugar, and nutmeg. The pastry is then topped with honey or a syrup flavored with lemon, orange, or cinnamon. Since baklava is so rich and sweet, only very small pieces are served at a time.

Thicker sheets of phyllo are used to make *pita*, a folded bread that is served warm or at room temperature. Like the Middle Eastern product of the same name, pita is usually stuffed with meat, vegetables, sweets, or other ingredients.

Dolmades and Moussaka

One favorite treat in Greece is *dolmades*, or stuffed grape leaves. Greeks have been using grape leaves to wrap food for thousands of years. The leaves are usually picked fresh in the spring and summer but can be preserved in olive oil and salt for use year-round.

Grape leaves to be used in cooking are dipped in water and laid out flat. Then fillings of different types, perhaps rice or vegetables, are placed in the middle. The bottom is folded up

Dolmades are grape leaves stuffed with rice or vegetables.

and then the sides are folded in to form a tube. A row of stuffed grape leaves is laid in a baking dish, then covered in broth and lemon sauce. When the dish has finished baking, it is served with lemon slices and a spoonful of yogurt.

Another Greek favorite is *moussaka*, the national dish, which was brought to the country hundreds of years ago from France. This popular entrée is made of layers of eggplant, potatoes, onions, red peppers, and slices of lamb. It is served in a cooked white sauce of butter, milk, and flour called *béchamel*, which was part of the original French recipe.

Time for a Snack

Because the Greeks tend to go many hours between sit-down meals, they often enjoy snacks in between. Some of the most

A favorite Greek dish is moussaka, which is prepared with layers of eggplant, lamb, potatoes, and other ingredients.

popular snacks are simple, including sardines, olives, fried cheese, meatballs, eggplant paste, grilled octopus, and fried zucchini. Another favorite is *souvlaki*, or meat on a stick. Typically lamb is put on a **skewer**, brushed in lemon juice and olive oil, and placed over an open fire until cooked through. After being removed from the skewer, the lamb is put on a plate and garnished with grilled onions and tomatoes, along

Skewered lamb kebabs are served with tzatziki, a tasty yogurt sauce.

Spanakokeftedes

This is similar to the traditional Greek spanakopita but easier because it doesn't call for phyllo. Instead of spinach pie, this recipe makes spinach balls—about two dozen in all. You will need an adult to help with the steaming and frying.

Ingredients

2 pounds fresh spinach

3 eggs

3 tablespoons melted butter

1 cup grated Parmesan cheese

½ cup crumbled feta cheese

½ cup minced dill

Salt and pepper to taste

1 cup bread crumbs

Vegetable oil (for frying)

Directions

Wash and clean the spinach leaves, but do not drain. Pull off the stems and place the leaves in a large sauce-pan. Cover and steam over high heat until the spinach is wilted. This will take about 3 minutes. Have an adult drain the spinach, and chop it up.

Mix in the eggs, butter, cheeses, dill, salt, and pepper. Shape the mixture into one-inch balls. Roll each ball in bread crumbs. Have an adult deep-fry the balls in hot oil. As each ball is removed from the oil, set it to drain on sheets of paper towels. Serve warm.

with some homemade bread on the side. Often souvlaki is topped with *tzatziki*, a creamy sauce made out of yogurt, garlic, diced cucumbers, olive oil, and mint leaves.

One of the sweetest and most unique snacks in all of Greece is known as "spoon sweets." They are often made out of sour cherries, grapes, and figs. They are served in jars much like fruit jelly or preserves. Some people eat them with a spoon— which is how the treat got its name. Others put the spoon of sweetness in a glass of cold water and stir it until it dissolves and they can drink it.

A sweet treat found in Greece is something called spoon sweets.

Many of the most popular recipes in Greece are based on holiday and religious beliefs. Certain dishes are made to celebrate holidays—from Name Day and Christmas to the most important holiday of the year in Greece—Easter!

FOUR

The Role of Religion

From one end of the country to the other, religion is important to the Greeks. All but 2 or 3 percent of the people share the same religion. They are members of the Greek Orthodox Church, a form of Catholicism distinct from that of the Roman Catholic Church and the churches in the Anglican Communion. Not only does belonging to this Catholic community affect how the Greeks live their lives, it also has an influence on how they cook and eat.

The Catholic religion has many important feast days, and in Greece, almost every single one is celebrated with some kind of special food. Although Name Day, Christmas, and New Year's Day are big holidays throughout the country, the most preparation and the most cooking and baking go into the proper celebration of Easter.

Carnival!

For many Catholics around the world, Easter is the most important feast day. This is certainly true throughout Greece.

Welcoming a Baby

When a baby is born to a Greek family, it's traditional to plant an olive tree in the child's honor. Some folk stories advise the parents of a baby girl to put a rolling pin in her crib to encourage her to grow up to be a talented phyllo maker.

Because baptism is such an important Christian sacrament, a baby's baptism day is cause for celebration. Usually the baby, who has not been given a name until now, is undressed and wrapped in a white cloth or towel. The infant is then dipped in water that contains olive oil and blessed by the priest with "myrrh"— more olive oil. A feast follows at the home of the parents or at a local restaurant.

Whether on the mainland, the peninsula, or one of the many islands, preparation for Easter begins weeks ahead of the actual day. Family members often return home from other parts of Greece or even other countries to share the holiday together.

Three weeks before **Lent** begins, the Greeks celebrate *Apokries*, or Carnival. The event usually begins toward the end of February or in early March, but the date changes from one year to the next because the date of Easter is different each year. Carnival is a long party, full of fun and feasting. In the first week, meat is served far more often than usual, especially roast

A couple roast their Easter lamb in the traditional manner, over outdoor coals.

pig or lamb. The meat is frequently cooked outdoors over open pits for 3 to 5 hours. It is rubbed with lemon juice and olive oil. As the cooking proceeds, the aroma spreads throughout the village or city, making people's mouths water and their stomachs rumble. People are encouraged to eat as much as they want, since Lent, a time of fasting, is just around the corner.

During the second week, Greeks celebrate Burnt Thursday or *tsiknopempti*, in which food is intentionally burned or charred over large, hot fires. The smell fills the air and adds to the spirit of the day. This is the last day for eating meat, so families often

Rizogalo (Rice Pudding)

This light dessert is the perfect ending to a Greek meal. Be sure to ask an adult to help with the boiling part.

Ingredients

- 2 cups water
- ½ cup long-grain rice
- 1 quart milk
- 2 egg yolks
- 1 cup sugar
- ½ teaspoon salt
- Ground cinnamon

Directions

Have an adult bring water to a boil on the stove top. Add the rice. Simmer, covered, for 15 to 20 minutes. Add the milk, making sure not to let it boil over. Continue to cook, stirring the pudding often for about 30 minutes. It is done when the rice is soft and the mixture is quite thick. Remove from the heat and set aside.

Beat egg yolks and sugar until they are thick and pale in color. Slowly stir the rice mixture into the beaten egg yolk mixture. Combine the ingredients thoroughly and return the pudding to the saucepan. Add salt and cook over low heat for an additional 2 minutes, stirring constantly to prevent curdling. Pour the mix into pudding dishes and sprinkle with cinnamon. This dessert can be served immediately, while it is warm—or put in the refrigerator and served later, cold.

spend the entire day dining together at home or heading out to a restaurant. During the third week, no meat is eaten and instead, most people consume cheese, fruits, and vegetables. The carnival ends with the burning of the Carnival King. People set fire to a paper statue of Judas, then set off fireworks and feast for hours into the night.

Lent

The sixth Monday before Easter is considered the first day of Lent. Typically during Lent, Catholics fast, or limit food intake, as a sacrifice. In Greece, this often means eating no meat. In Greece the first day of Lent is called "Clean Monday." The people have big outdoor feasts that feature delicious vegetarian dishes. They use different types of seafood such as octopus and shrimp, plus eggs, cheese, and olives. Bean stews, salads, rice dishes, and dolmades are made and shared. As people eat and chat, the skies are often filled with colorful kites, a traditional part of the celebration.

The week before Easter begins is known as Holy Week. One of the traditional foods prepared during this holiday is red-dyed eggs, or *kokkina avga*. In Greece, instead of painting or dyeing eggs in different colors and patterns for the holiday as in some countries, all the eggs are dyed red on the Thursday before Easter. Although some stores sell the dye, many families color their eggs the old-fashioned way using onion skins to dye the shells. The bright red eggs are then polished with olive oil until they shine

Easter bread includes bright red-dyed eggs.

and either displayed on kitchen tables in homes or in front windows in shops and stores. Many are given as gifts to family and friends. Some of the eggs are added to a special Easter bread also. On Easter Sunday, the eggs are peeled and eaten, or used in children's games.

Good Friday and Easter

On the Friday before Easter, called Good Friday, many people throughout the country hang their flags at half-mast at home and at their businesses. Many Catholics spend the day fasting, taking in nothing other than water until midnight. The mood is somber as people think about what their faith means to them. Different areas throughout Greece have a procession in which a coffin is carried through the streets to represent the death of Jesus. At the end of the procession, the people return to their homes, carrying the candles they had used to light their way. Some set off fireworks at the stroke of midnight. There is an air of excitement and celebration now, and by the time Sunday morning arrives, everyone in Greece is ready for a day of feasting, fun, and family. Lamb is often prepared in casseroles, roasts, and soups. A variety of fancy and festive breads are baked and meals end with sticky desserts and strong coffee.

Other Holidays

While Easter is definitely the most important holiday in Greece celebrated with foods that have been traditional for centuries, Christmas, New Year's, and Name Day are among the other feast days associated with special types of food, with an emphasis on desserts.

Typically, Greeks do not eat many sweet desserts. If they choose a dessert at all, it is usually a piece of fruit. Pastries are popular but normally are eaten as a meal in themselves, rather than at the end of lunch or dinner. This set of habits certainly changes during the holidays. Cooks all over Greece work hard to create some of the most delicious treats in the world. From syrup cakes to Saint Basil's cakes, which contain a baked-in surprise, desserts are the source of some of the country's best recipes.

Syrup cakes are a big favorite with young and old alike. Those with a real sweet tooth like these treats. Typically, the cake itself is a simple yellow cake, although walnuts, almonds, orange rind, honey, cinnamon, or cloves may be added. When the batter has been baked, the cook pokes holes in the top and pours on a syrup, which seeps through the holes to spread throughout the cake. The syrup is usually made from orange blossoms, sour cherries, roses, or lemons—plus sugar, of course. Syrup cake is quite gooey and must be eaten with a spoon instead of a fork.

Baklava and spoon sweets are popular treats as well. In addition, Greeks are known for a variety of cookies such as *melomakaronas* (spiced honey cookies), *loukoumades* (fried honey puffs made with flour, lemon juice, and honey), and *kourambiedes* (sugar-coated cookies containing cloves and almonds and rolled in powdered sugar). Kourambiedes, a sign of happiness, are given out on holidays and at weddings. A different type of pastry made for New Year's, as well as for weddings and baptisms, is *diples*, which means

Traditional holiday cookies are prepared throughout Greece.

"double" in Greek. This light dessert, filled largely with air, is topped with honey and cinnamon. Often it is made in shapes like braids and bows.

Bread is another Greek treat. Sweet rings of bread are made for weddings and crosses at Christmas. Festive Greek breads are often baked with figs, oranges, almonds, walnuts, and sesame seeds inside of them. On New Year's Eve, many cooks make *vasilopita*, or the New Year pie. Made in honor of Saint Basil, a saint from the fourth century, this bread not only tastes good but has a surprise inside. Bakers place a gold coin inside each cake they make. At midnight, when the treat is traditionally served, everyone hopes to get the slice with the coin. According to the old belief, the lucky person will have wealth and good fortune throughout the coming year.

Going Caroling

In Greece, young children may go door to door during the Christmas season carrying and playing handheld instruments, such as triangles and bells. They knock on the door of a house and sing a Christmas carol to those who answer. In return, they are often given sweets, from slices of bread to cookies, cake, or pastries.

Sweet bread rings are made for weddings.

Happy Name Day

Because of their Catholic faith, the people of Greece often celebrate Name Day instead of an actual birthday. When babies are born, in addition to their individual names, they receive the name of a certain saint. They are not named for a parent but often carry the names of a grandparent and the area's patron saint. On the patron saint's feast day, everyone bearing that saint's name may have a party or open house and, of course, a feast is part of the celebration. Small gifts are given to the person as well. Occasionally, children will carry the name of a Greek philosopher as well, such as Socrates or Plato.

FIVE

Staying Healthy, Living Longer

|||||||||||||||||||||||||||||||||||||||||||||||||||||||||||||||||||||||||||||||||||||

The Greek diet includes many of the same ingredients found countrywide: olives and olive oil, nuts, garlic, vegetables, wild greens, fish, and grains. This style of eating is often called the

A diet rich in olives and olive oil, fresh vegetables, greens, fish, and grains is called a Mediterranean diet.

Reaching Triple Digits

One of the smallest and most remote islands in Greece is called Ikaria. It is only 99 square miles (256 sq km) in size, yet one-third of its population is ninety years old—or older. Not only do many Ikarians live for a century or more, but they also have a 20 percent lower risk of cancer, half the rate of heart disease, and one-ninth the rate of diabetes. Researchers believe that the reason for all this is a combination of diet, lower levels of stress, regular afternoon naps, and frequent exercise.

Mediterranean diet. Ask the people of Greece why they live such long lives, and they will happily give the credit to their diet. Medical research and studies have in fact lent support to this belief. A diet rich in many of the foods that the Greeks eat regularly has been shown to be very healthy. Some experts even believe this type of diet is the key to living longer.

Researchers have studied the Mediterranean diet for decades. Several years ago a group of researchers studied more than 214,000 men and more than 166,000 women over a period of ten years to see how this type of diet affected their health and life spans. They found a definite connection between higher levels of health, lower risk of disease, and increased **longevity**.

Arakas me Anitho
(Dilled Peas with Peppers)

This simple dish combines vegetables with Greece's favorite ingredient: olive oil. It is a wonderful side dish to go with meat and bread.

Ingredients

1 pound frozen peas
3 tablespoons dried dill weed
4 small onions, diced
1 green bell pepper, diced
1 red bell pepper, diced
1 cup olive oil
½ teaspoon salt
¾ cup water

Directions

With an adult's help, cut up the onions and peppers. Put them into a large saucepan, and add the peas, dill, olive oil, salt, and water.

Put a cover on the pan. Bring to a boil over high heat and then reduce heat to low. Cook for 30 minutes, and serve hot.

Greek Etiquette

Good manners for guests dining at a Greek home differ in several ways from etiquette in the United States. Getting there 30 minutes late is considered being on time, and guests should be sure to compliment the host and hostess on the appearance of the house. Guests are not supposed to sit down until they have been invited to, and they are not to start eating until the hostess has taken the first bite. Meal times are for socializing, so they tend to be loud and lively. They usually begin with a toast such as the familiar *Stinygiasou* or *Eis igian sas* (To Your Health) at more formal occasions. Having a second helping shows respect to the host, and guests who soak up the last bit of sauce with a piece of bread are showing extra appreciation.

A number of people believe that it is not just *what* the Greeks eat that keeps them healthier but *how* they eat it. Almost no one rushes through a meal. It is customary for people to take their time to enjoy their food. Lunch may last 2 to 3 hours from beginning to end, and dinner may last even longer. Eating alone is virtually unheard of. Instead, meals are spent with family and friends, chatting, socializing, and enjoying one another's company.

Three Greek men dine together. Sharing meals in an important part of Greek culture.

The combination of eating fresh, wholesome food slowly, in the company of people you care about, may be a key to living longer and staying healthier. For the people of Greece, it certainly seems to be the right answer—especially if it all comes with a bowl of olives and a sauce of olive oil and lemon juice!

Glossary

baptism a religious ceremony in which a person—in Greece, usually an infant—is admitted into the religious community by immersion in water and by blessing

cured soaked in brine (salty water)

Lent in Greece, the period between Clean Monday and Easter, usually observed by times of fasting

longevity length of life

marinating the soaking of a food in a sauce

monastery a house or enclosed community occupied by monks under religious vows

peninsula an area of land that is almost completely surrounded by water

shortening butter, lard, or some other form of fat

siesta a short period of rest, usually in the middle of the afternoon

skewer a long pin of wood or metal for inserting through pieces of meat or other foods to hold them during cooking, often over a grill or open fire

Find Out More

BOOKS

Gifford, Clive. *Food and Cooking in Ancient Greece*. New York: Powerkids Press, 2010.

Locricchio, Matthew. *The Cooking of Greece*. New York: Benchmark Books, 2012.

Sheen, Barbara. *Foods of Greece*. New York: KidHaven Press, 2006.

DVDS

The Beauties of Greece, Paul Pissanos Productions, 2010.

Beautiful Greece (Best of Europe), Small World Productions, 2010.

WEBSITES

Ancient Greece

http://greece.mrdonn.org/

Learn all about ancient Greek culture, from maps and geography to daily life and sports.

Food in Ancient Greece

www.historyforkids.org/learn/greeks/food/greekfood.htm

This site includes discussion of food in ancient Greece for kids that tells the meaning behind the dishes.

Peoples and Places: Greece

http://kids.nationalgeographic.com/kids/places/find/greece/

At this website, discover Greek geography, history, people, culture, and more. Interactive videos, maps, and ecards are also available.

Index

Page numbers in **boldface** are illustrations and charts.

About the Author

Tamra Orr is a full-time writer and author living in the Pacific Northwest. She has written more than 250 nonfiction books for readers of all ages and has traveled the world through her writing. As a mother of four, she shares everything she learns with her children. An avid reader and letter writer, she has a degree in secondary education and English from Ball State University in Muncie, Indiana.